C000144164

Curious
COYOTE

Ellen Haas &
Lexie Bakewell

ZieBee Media

PORTLAND, OREGON, USA

Curious
COYOTE

Written by
Ellen Haas & Lexie Bakewell

This book is a tool for people who want to spark curiosity in the natural world, bring nature into their everyday life, and be inspired by nature as they explore their imagination.

Copyright 2018 © Ellen Haas, Lexie Bakewell, and Mackenzie Bakewell

All Rights Reserved.
First Printing Fall 2020.

Edited by Mackenzie Bakewell

Designed & Published by ZieBee Media - *ZieBee.com*

Photographs by:
    Aaron Baggenstos - *AaronBaggenstos.com*
    ZieBee Media - *ZieBee.com*

Cover Photograph from *www.Fotolia.com*

ISBN 978-1-7358507-1-9

See more from the authors at:
ZieBee.com/Coyote

ZieBee Media
PORTLAND, OREGON, USA

Curious COYOTE

Nature Breaks that build a stronger connection with nature, by helping you to expand your awareness and open your senses.

Welcome to Coyote's Curiosity

This little book is a sidekick to *Coyote's Pocket Guide to Connecting Kids with Nature*. It jump-starts you into creating and developing your own Nature Connection practice. It offers prompts - questions, missions and challenges - that brighten awareness.

Each section has its own title and color, and emphasizes a different Core Routine that enhances nature connection.

What I Love: expressing gratitude

Magical Senses: awakening sensory awareness

Being Wild: charades and imitations

Find: scavenger hunts

Journaling: writing and sketching

Thrival: survival challenges

Sit Spot: still, quiet and alone activities

Stories: sharing experiences and feelings

Whether you are at a Sit Spot, on a Wander, or pausing for Thanksgiving, this collection of prompts helps you, the Coyote Mentor, to playfully entice children into making connections with nature.

Allow these examples to spark your imagination in creating your own questions, activities, and quests as you plunge into becoming a naturally curious and playful Coyote Mentor.

Directions for Use:

1. Choose one of the Core Routines of Nature Connection to emphasize.

2. Pick a page or two to work with and explore what it says.

3. Use whichever suggestions best fit your site and situation.

4. Allow our words to inspire your own variations.

5. Follow the energies of the Natural Cycle to aid in selecting your activities.

What I Love

Earth

**Give thanks for the
planet that is our home.**

Rocks are at the core
of everything that is.

Which parts of you feel rocky?
Earth's hills and valleys
shape many different homes
for all kinds of beings.

**In what type of landscape
do you feel most at home?**

*What do you love about
the Earth?*

What I Love

Water

Give thanks for the waters that flow.

Water softly fills our blood,
cleans the air, and
levels mountains.

Water takes many forms:
rain, snow clouds, rivers,
waves, glaciers, tears...

What forms can you see around you right now?

What do you love about the Waters?

What I Love

Plants

Give thanks for the plants that grow everywhere.

How do you use plants?
Plants change sunlight
into food, medicine, fuel,
and even your clothes.

What plant stands out to you?
Flowers are thought of as
the Earth's laughter.

Are any laughing right now?

***What do you love about
the Plants?***

What I Love

Animals

**Give thanks for the
animals who are our kin.**

Animals come in all types,
mice, hawks, and elephants,
pets and wild neighbors.

Which animal are you like?
They move, eat, mate
and depend on each other.

**What animals do
you depend on?**

*What do you love about
the Animals?*

What I Love

Trees

**Give thanks for trees in
woodlands, orchards,
and your neighborhood.**

How do you use trees daily?
Trees give us fire, shade, food
and the air we breathe.
Pencils, juice, toilet paper?
Old, tall, rooted trees
shelter whole communities
and reach for the sun.

Who lives in your trees?

***What do you love about
the Trees?***

What I Love

Birds

**Give thanks for the birds
who soar and sing.**

Birds are everywhere.
Way up high, hidden in a bush,
feathers on the ground.

Can you spot one now?

Their voices and actions
tell us many stories.

**Can you tell if they are
happy or alarmed?**

*What do you love about
the Birds?*

What I Love

Weather

**Give thanks for the
ever-changing weather.**

Sun, clouds and rain shift...
hot to cold,
wet to dry,
still to windy.

What's the weather like today?
Dramatic storms give stories to tell.

**Can you remember ones
you have lived through?**

***What do you love about
the Weather?***

What I Love

Sun

Give thanks that the earth turns toward the sun each day.

Sunlight feeds most every
living thing.

**How do you eat the
sun's energy?**

The sun can feel sweetly soft,
fiercely hot, wetly sticky.

What is its mood today?

Have you seen a sunrise or
sunset that was magical?

*What do you love about
the Sun?*

Magical Senses

Sense of Direction

**A horse can find it's way home.
So can you!**

**What direction are you
facing right now?**

Look to where the sun rises and
sets to know east and west.
Notice landmarks and build a
mental image of your route.

**Can you travel off trail
and find your way back?**

*Use a compass to check how
well you are doing.*

Magical Senses

Owl Eyes

Owl eyes notice everything.
Soften your eyes, gaze widely
to the rim of your vision.

Notice where....
darkness hides
brightness shines
colors stand out
shadows shift
Be the owl.
Still on a branch,
eyes broadly focused
alert to any little stirring
that might mean prey.

Dart your focus to that spot.

Magical Senses

Raccoon Hands

Raccoons find their food by feeling with their fingertips.

Close your eyes and run
your hand over rough bark,
dig your fingers into damp soil.

Explore textures that are...
  rough as rocks
  soft as down
  fuzzy as caterpillars
  prickly as thorns
  slippery as slugs

Which is more sensitive, your fingertip, cheek, or tongue?

Magical Senses

Dog Nose

Dogs' noses smell the stories
of those who have passed by.
Draw breath through your nose.
What aromas float on the air?

Get close and smell....
dank mud
leaf litter
wet dog
Lift your nose and smell...
coming storm
tangy smoke
sweet flowers

Can you smell more facing
upwind or downwind?

Magical Senses

Deer Ears

Deer listen by rotating their tall ears back and forth.

Close your eyes and cup your ears to make big deer ears.
Cup them forward.
Cup them backward.

Does this change how you hear?

Who is making noise?
How many different sounds?
Where are the sounds from?

Can you draw a map of the sounds that surround you?

Magical Senses

Snake Taste

**Snakes flick their tongues
to taste what's on the air.**

**Where on your tongue
can you taste....**
salty, sweet, sour, bitter?

Bitter tastes on the back of
your tongue so you can
retch up poisonous things
before swallowing.

Taste a snack that you carry.
What type of taste is it?
Where it is on your tongue?

Find words that for different tastes.

Magical Senses

Blind Sensing

Humans do most of their sensing with their eyes. Shut your eyes.

Can you feel...
the sun on your face
the ground underfoot

Can you hear...
the breeze in the trees
the birds calling out

Can you smell...
the dampness in the air
the scent of crushed grass.

*Without vision, let your
other senses wake up.*

Magical Senses

Cat Radar

**Cats are watchful and wary,
tuned in to possibilities.**

They pause in the shadows, sniff,
look up, down, around, then
choose a direction to go.

Move like a cat.
Stop, open your senses.
Listen to your body.

Go where you feel...
a pull, a tingle, an inkling,
an idea, or a sense of attraction.

Where do you end up?

Being Wild

Animal Dramas

**Nature is full of drama,
comedy, tragedy, story.**

Animal dramas….
  goats butt heads
  shorebirds move as one
  wolves take down a deer
  birds fight in the air
  spiders wrap up their prey
  sharks chase surfers
  lemmings jump off cliffs
  gulls squabble over fish guts

*With partners, improvise
an Animal Drama.*

Being Wild

Traveling Rocks

Earth is alive and active.
Mountains rise, rocks crack,
soil erodes.

Imagine Earth stretching...
    rocks tumble off cliffs
    volcanoes explode violently
    earthquakes shake and crack
    landslides melt hillsides
    sandstorms shift dunes
    pebbles race downstream

Imagine that rocks enjoy
flexing their muscles.

Pretend to be rocks on the move.

Being Wild

Playful Water

Water flows playfully,
in sky, land and sea.

Water shape-shifts as...
    flying clouds
    pounding hailstorms
    blinding blizzards
    crashing waves
    whirling waterspouts
    dripping icicles
    blood in your veins

Imagine being water,
what shape would you take?

Act out water moving.

Being Wild

Unfurling Greens

**Plants are rooted, but still reach
out stems, leaves, and flowers.**

Plants move as...
    seeds swelling
    sprouts breaking ground
    fronds unfurling
    buds blossoming
    stems multiplying
    vines climbing
    grasses waving in the wind

**Can you imagine
their daily changes?**

Imitate a plant growing.

Being Wild

Shifting Shapes

Animals are mobile and move every which way.

Animals move differently...
Frogs leap
Snakes slither
Inchworms hunch
Cats stalk
Owls glide
Deer bound
Whales spy-hop
Coyotes pounce

Imitate an animal moving.

Imagine moving like it all day.

Being Wild

Tree Homes

**Trees stand rooted,
and shelter lots of life.**

Who lives in trees?
  birds perch and sing
  squirrels stash nuts
  woodpeckers drill holes
  beetles etch under bark
  raccoons den in cavities
  bats hang in hollows
  snakes lounge on limbs

**A fallen tree harbors more life than
a living one.**

Imitate a tree's network of life.

Being Wild

Flying Dancers

**Birds have wide wings and
light bones so they can fly.**

Birds move in many ways...
> Kingfishers dive into water
> Eagles soar in circles
> Hummingbirds hover
> Penguins swim
> Woodpeckers drum
> Herons spear fish
> Flycatchers snag bugs

**All birds sing, call, beg,
and squawk in alarm.**

Imitate a bird you like.

Being Wild

Startling Wind

The wind is invisible but can still be seen.

Wind leaves its tracks in...
swaying trees
billowing clouds
spinning dust devils
twirling leaves
riffling water
blowing sand
drifting dandelion fluffs

**How can you see the wind?
What sounds is it making?**

Imitate moving wind.

Find

Pretty Rocks

As you wander
gather rocks that call to you.

Collect stones that are...
    perfectly round
    sharp and jagged
    smooth and polished
    sparkly or gleaming
    striped or lined
    multi-colored
    cracked in two

Close your eyes.
Feel the stone, smell it.
Hold it tight in your hand.

How is it like you?

Find

Discover Leaves

**As you wander
look for different leaves.**

Gather leaves that have...
jagged edges
animal chews
a heart shape
signs of disease
a furry side
parallel veins
a long skinny shape

How was it attached?

*Which is your favorite?
Why do you like it?*

Find

Rainbow Colors

**As you wander
admire colors everywhere.**

**Find all the colors
of the rainbow.**
red, orange, yellow,
green, blue, purple,
even black and white.

Look for colors in:
flowers, leaves, rocks,
bark, birds, beetles, dirt, sky.

Can you find 5 different greens?

Which colors are hardest to find?

Find

Textures

As you wander
explore with your fingers.

Feel textures that are...
rough and sharp
prickly and painful
fuzzy and soft
smooth and silky
sticky and slimy
scaly and dry

Does it feel different
if you close your eyes?

What does this texture
remind you of?

Find

Animal Homes

**As you wander
search for animal homes.**

Look up, down, and in...
    nests - high and low
    holes in the ground
    webs everywhere
    beds in thickets
    cavities in trees
    hideaways under shrubs
    under rocks and leaves

Who lives there? Is anyone home?

*If you were out in the wild what
type of home would you build?*

Find

Oxymoron

As you wander
find opposite traits
in the same thing.

Find one thing that is both...
young and old
dead and alive
weak yet strong
soft and hard
still but moving
delicate but dangerous

A tree can be dead and alive.
A spider delicate but dangerous.

How might you be oxymoronic?

Find

Variations

As you wander
discover differences in
things that are similar.

See if you can find...
different shaped leaves
different tree barks
different types of grasses
different colored flowers
different tiny animals

What makes these alike? What
makes them look different?

*Can you tell them apart
with your eyes closed?*

Find

Catchables

**As you wander
hunt for small animals.**

Look closely....
        into flower blossoms
        under cool rocks
        in still water
        inside rotting wood
        in the crevices of bark
        under leaf litter

**Can you catch them gently?
Please return them home.**

*When you release them,
what do they do?*

Journaling

Quick Check-In

**Start every journal page
with a quick heading.**

When?
    Monday, January 5, 5:45
    Late in day, sun setting

Where?
    Open field near big tree

Weather?
    Still, breath showing cold

What's happening?
    Treetop hawk watches

***Notice how this record
changes over time.***

Journaling

Looking Closely

**Sketch to stick an image
in your imagination.**

Find something living.
Look closely and carefully
at all its amazing details.

Look away.
Draw it from memory.

Look again.
Add what you missed.

Repeat.
Look, look away, sketch...

*Notice shapes, textures, and
how the parts connect.*

Journaling

Field Notes

**Keep inventory
of your adventures.**

Earth mud slide in ravine
Water rivers flooded
Plants daffodil opening
Animals first spring peepers
Trees wild apples flowering
Birds two crows fighting
Weather foggy and silent
Sun subtle glow in mist
Night sky full moon

*Record highlights
where they fit.*

Journaling

Onomatopoeia

**Spell words that imitate
sounds you hear.**

Animals: ribbit, purrr, oink buzz,
yip-yip-yip, grrrr, moo
Weather: kaboom, splatter, splash,
pitter-patter, whoosh
Trees: wooahh, creak, clak-clak,
chatter, rustle, sigh
Birds: tweet, quack, ratitat-tat,
whoo, chick-a-dee-dee

This is onomatopoeia!

*Write words that sound
like a sound sounds.*

Journaling

Spirit Sketches

**See like an artist
But draw just a little sketch.**

Capture the spirit of an object
by drawing quick, sweeping lines.

Attitude: curled sleeping cat
Posture: tall waiting heron
Texture: prickly bush
Pattern: leaf veins and bark
Shape: plump winter bird
Action: leaping reaching frog

*Does your sketch capture
a glimpse of what you saw?*

Journaling

Mapping

**Map the route you
traveled today.**

**On a big piece of paper draw a
circle with the four directions.**
North, East, South, West

Locate on this map
all the important
roads, pathways, animal trails,
waterways, hills and valleys, trees
and fields, landmarks.
Check in with others.

*Sketch in bubble stories
of your best encounters.*

Journaling

Ruminations

Reflect on something that touched or surprised you.

Remember your experience.
Visualize it. Relive it.
What was interesting about it?

Go over the details.
Ask why it happened.
Poke it with all your senses.
What emotions did you feel?
What were you thinking?
Write the story down.

Can you describe it so others will feel how you felt?

Journaling

Best Words

**Have fun choosing new words
to best express your thoughts.**

Instead of awesome was it
thrilling, magical, stunning,
powerful, fearsome?

Instead of interesting was it
curious, odd, exciting, different?

Instead of pretty was it
ornate, colorful, graceful, sparkly?

Instead of broken was it
rotted twisted, shattered, cracked?

*Hunt for the perfect words that
say exactly what you mean.*

Thrival

Predator/Prey

**Do you want to eat or
do you fear being eaten?**
Either way, wear
a Cloak of Invisibility.

Blend in.
Avoid shouty clothes, mud up
your face, cover your smell.

Be still and quiet.
Empty your thoughts
of fear or excitement.

**Stay in the shadows
and move with stealth.**

(make no disturbance)

Thrival

Track an Animal

Are wild animals nearby?
Hunt them.

Study the toes of footprints
in mud puddles and sand.
Count the claw marks.

Follow trails
through underbrush to matted
grasses where deer lay.

Decipher signs...
chews, poops, scratchings,
pathways, burrows and nests.

Follow their clues to discover
who was here recently.

Thrival

Go Fishing

Hungry? Creek nearby?
Make your way to a place by
water where fish may live.

When would they be hungry?
What would they like to eat?

Watch carefully for ripples
where fish jump.
Toss crumbs to attract
their attention.

Be patient. Settle in. Sit still.

Who else is coming
to the water to fish?

Thrival

Find Water

Thirsty? Dirty?

Scan your landscape.
Study it on a contour map.
Find where water runs.
down slopes and into valleys.
Where does it pool?
Wherever water collects,
plants and animals thrive.

Find water!
Slurp water off a leaf.
Gather rainwater in a shell.
Boil creek water to make it safe.

To wash up, lay down in a creek!

Thrival

Take Shelter

Pouring rain? Scorching sun?
Take shelter!

Where do animals hide?
In safe, dry, cozy places.

Find shelter.
In the bushes
under trees
against rocks
inside hollow logs
protected from the wind
shaded from the sun.

Get inside. Get comfy.
Make a nest and feel snug.

Thrival

Lost & Found

Wandering off trail?
Here's how to stay found.

Study your surroundings and
make a map in your mind.
Notice major landmarks.
Big rock, tall tree,distant peak,
creek crossing, roaring river.

Turn around often to
imprint your return route.
Keep track of the time so you
know when to turn back.

Make up a story to recall
the path you traveled.

Thrival

Thrive with Art

**Art feeds the spirit and
helps people to blossom.**

**Nature provides all
the materials you need.**
Explore color, contrast, patterns.
Collect and arrange leaves,
seed pods, sticks, bones, stones.
Braid grasses and flower stems.
Tie things together to hang.

**Make temporary designs,
patterns, and collages.**

*Create an art show and
share your art with others.*

Thrival

Make a Fire

Need warmth? Want to cook?
Make a fire.

Gather, in separate piles:
- Tinder: tiny dry twigs, grass,
  needles, cones, wood slivers.
- Kindling: dry sticks, wide as a
  finger, long as a forearm.
- Fuel wood: thicker branches.

A fire needs air and fuel.
Lay the firewood
so your spark will catch
on tiny tinder then grow bigger.

Watch how flame eats wood.

Sit Spot

Magnify

**See the extraordinary
in the ordinary.**
Look closely at something
little until it becomes big.

Magnify....
the underside of leaves
the patterns in bark
the colors in a flower
the pictures in a drop of water

**How does this new world look
like something else you know?
How does it make you feel?**

What about it surprises you?

Sit Spot

Solo

You are alone,
yet life is all around you.
If there is any fear, feel it as
the edge of adventure.

Breathe deep.
Use your dog nose.

Listen all around.
Use your deer ears.

The earth and her wild ones
send their greetings
in subtle and curious ways.

Notice.
And greet them back.

Sit Spot

Bird Language

Birds are nature's tattle-tales.

Sit quietly, patiently,
listen as they start talking.

**What could their little
chirps mean?**
Are they checking-in, cheery,
begging, bossy, gossipy?

Are they nervous and alarmed?
Suddenly quiet, scolding, flying up
and away or down to cover?

Watch their behavior.

What are they saying to you?

Sit Spot

Scent of Water

**Some people can smell
rain coming.**

**Can you smell any trace
of moisture in the air?**
Can your skin feel humidity?
Is it wet beneath your seat?

Do you hear any water sounds?
dripping, pattering, lapping,
gurgling, hissing?

**Are there any pockets or drops of
water within your reach?**

How might animals sense water?

Sit Spot

Hiding

You have startled the neighborhood.

Camouflage yourself.
Still your body.
Quiet your thinking.
Slow your breathing.
Widen your vision.
Listen in all directions.

**Many are still here,
hidden and watching.**
Become the watcher, too.

*If you sit quietly, the animals will
come to you with curiosity.*

Sit Spot

Who's There

Look closely for the small overlooked animals.
Worms, spiders, bees, beetles, butterflies, mites, caterpillars, millipedes, slugs, newts.

Who is busily moving?

Notice what it is doing.
Does it have legs?
How many?
What is its face like?
Does it use antennae?

How is it like you?
How are you like it?

Sit Spot

Ceremony

**Simple ceremonies honor
your oneness with nature.**

At your Sit Spot,
gather special things you have
collected and place them in a
graceful and artistic way.

Clear your mind
Open your senses
Breathe

**Enjoy your surroundings.
Feel at home in nature.**

Say why you are happy.

Sit Spot

Messengers

**Plants and animals
can bring you messages.**
Pay attention when something
catches your eye.

Look twice.
What is interesting about it?
Is it doing something unusual?
Is it communicating with you?

Ask it, have a chat
What comes into your mind?
What can you learn from it?

*Listen for the still small voice
What do you hear?*

Stories

Fear

**Tell a story of when
you were really scared.**

Were you...
> lost?
> cold and wet?
> in a storm?
> too close to an edge?
> near a scary animal?
> alone in the dark?

**How have you
escaped danger?**

*Re-live your fear as you tell your
story so others feel it too.*

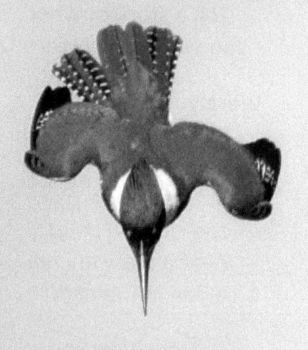

Stories

Agility

Tell a story of feeling as agile as a wild animal.

Were you...
    fighting and fleeing?
    stalking and pouncing?
    balancing on a log?
    crossing a fast creek?
    climbing up a tree?
    swinging on a vine?

Maybe you soared like an eagle or dashed like a rabbit.

What can your body do when you push its limits?

Stories

Curiosity

**Tell a story of something
that makes you curious.**

Is it...

dazzling and colorful?
out of place?
funny-looking?
a mysterious footprint?
moving strangely?
creepy?
surprising or astonishing?

Investigate it.

What details intrigue you?
What does it make you wonder?

Stories

Discomfort

Tell a story of when you were uncomfortable.

Did you feel...
    out of your comfort zone?
    attacked by thorns?
    humid and buggy?
    pushed too hard?
    awkward or clumsy?
    stuck in a small space?
    all alone or left out?

How did you survive?

What disturbed your comfort today? What did you do about it?

Stories

Death

Tell a story of being near a death.

Have you seen a...
>   tree fallen in the wind?
>   plant thirsty for water?
>   insect trapped in a web?
>   dried up worm?
>   a recent roadkill?

**Look for something
dead or dying today.**

**Have you ever held something
still alive but dying?**

How did it make you feel?

Stories

Awesome

**Tell a story of something
that struck you with awe.**

Was it....
> huge and filled the sky?
> tiny and up close?
> scary and shocking?
> musical and enchanting?
> wonderful to touch?
> inspiring in spirit?

Did it make you stop still stunned?

*Use vivid words to convey what
wowed you today.*

Stories

Obstacles

**Tell a story of
overcoming an obstacle.**

Have you ever met a....
tree growing out of rock?
creek plugged by landslide?
fish swimming upstream?
insect at a dead end?
baby bird learning to fly?
turtle on its back?

**What challenges have you faced;
what problems have you solved?**

Did it raise your confidence?

Stories

Darkness

**Tell a story of being outside
in the dark of night.**

Were you....
> without a flashlight?
> bathed in moonlight?
> aware of glowing eyes?
> feeling with your feet?
> startled by night noises?
> circled around a fire?

**Did your senses come on high alert?
Did they adjust?**

*Who else was out there with you
moving freely in the night?*

Natural Cycle
The Flowing Activities

	Activity	**Season**	**Time**	**Mood**
East	Greet & Gather	Spring	Sunrise	Inspiring
SE	Energize Awareness		Morning	Motivating
South	Foray	Summer	Midday	Focusing
SW	Wander		Afternoon	Relaxing
West	Show & Tell	Fall	Sunset	Congregating
NW	Still, Quiet, Alone		Dusk	Reflecting
North	Ceremony	Winter	Midnight	Integrating
NE	Home Base		Dawn	Regenerating

Excerpts from Coyote's Pocket Guide to Connecting Kids with Nature.

Cultivate Core Routines

1. **Sit Spot:** The practice of sitting in nature regularly at the same place.

2. **Story of the Day:** Sharing your finds and recounting the highlights of your day.

3. **Expanding Awareness:** Quieting your mind by awakening and expanding your senses.

4. **Imitating Animals:** Imagining and acting out animals' movements and behavior.

5. **Questioning & Tracking:** Looking for clues and asking questions to learn more about mysteries you encounter.

6. **Wandering:** Taking time to wander with no agenda, to follow your curiosity.

7. **Mapping & Orienting:** Paying attention to the directions, creating maps and knowing where you are in the landscape.

8. **Field Guides:** Browsing and searching to identify and learn about things that capture your attention.

9. **Keeping Journals:** Regularly recording your experiences in a journal by drawing, mapping and writing.

10. **Survival:** Practicing basic survival skills and techniques.

11. **Mind's Eye Imagining:** Looking deeply to create a mental image to use later.

12. **Listening for Bird Language:** Learning the tones of voice and erratic behaviors of birds to better understand what is going on in the landscape.

13. **Thanksgiving:** Expressing gratitude for the abundance, beauty, and presence of the natural world and all who live in it.

Nature is Calling...
Let's Go Outside & Play

See more from the authors at:
ZieBee.com/Coyote

ZieBee Media
PORTLAND, OREGON, USA

Lightning Source UK Ltd.
Milton Keynes UK
UKHW022024090122
396881UK00006B/27